Social media marketing 2017

The definitive guide to grow your social media following

Table of content

Introduction-

I want to thank you and congratulate you for downloading the book, "*Social media marketing*".

Social media platforms like Facebook, Twitter, Instagram or LinkedIn make it almost effortless for business to create and post content for a potential audience of billions. The biggest advantage is that is faster and cheaper than large-scale publishing, and also the most important thing, it's free.

The most important question that you can ask is: "Can I really make money with social media?" I got some good news for you. Yes, you can definitely you can make money with social media, nowadays a lot of people are making money with social media and it's more simple than you think if you follow the right plan and the right strategy.

Running a good social media campaign is a matter of a clear set of objectives, strategies, and tactics. The most important thing I don't consider to be the right tactics but the right mindset and set of beliefs. This book is written to help you to make sense of the madness, to make everything clear about this subject.

Thanks again for downloading this book. It will represent the best source that you need for learning social media marketing to the ultimate level. I hope you enjoy it!

Chapter 1 - What is social media and how powerful is today in your business?

At the end of this chapter you will know:

- What is social media and how to to use it
- What influences people and what makes them share news
- Creating an attractive and effective social media plan
- How to grow your business using social media and what strategies to apply

What is social media and is it necessary?

From time to time I hear people saying " I have no time for social media" , " I don't know how to use social media", "Social media it's complicated" to which I respond clearly that if you don't have time for it or you consider social media complicated then I can say without any doubts that you don't have time for marketing also and you are not preoccupied to create a relationship with your customer.

Social Media definition after Wikipedia is the fallowing "**Social media** are computer-mediated technologies that allow the creating and sharing of information, ideas, career interests and other forms of expression via virtual communities and networks." Source: Wikipedia. I would better describe social media as being a channel that you use to establish a connection with your customer, to inform him and to attract him.

Yes, you will have to put the effort in it, and yes will take time, but will pay off for sure. You may think that customers may not use social media for the type of business that you are running right now, nothing worst than that. Jumping into Social Media can be a game changer for you, clients nowadays are using more social media than ever. A VERY IMPORTANT aspect it's also how they consume their content on social media. Most of the prospects are using mobile devices like smartphones, tablets, watches, laptops. Obviously, the most used ones are smartphones for their small dimensions and portability.

Did you know that the fastest social media platform is Facebook and here over 60% are females? How cool is the fact that we can measure all demographics related to the location, sex, age and so on. How awesome would be to get customers feedback in real time to determine how to improve your product or service based on their needs and desires.

How are you marketing right now in your business?

Well, lets take a look at your marketing tools. I'm pretty sure that for the moment you are using your e-mail, you are using your website, articles, some offline sources of marketing like TV ads(maybe not even that), radio, newsletters and phone agenda, surveys. Let's take one by one, not only that those type of tools are a little bit outdated and not used anymore but one of the biggest disadvantages it's represented by the price and that impact that it makes. First of all your target audience may not be in from of the TV, may not using the radio anymore(probably no), your target audience may be between 18-24 years old so for sure they use the most computers and smartphones. Advertising on TV can be very expensive, and the return may not cover even the investment. Social media on the other side it's pretty simple to use and very friendly when it comes to creating ads. The budget that you need can be very small and make a splash in the industry that you are in right now. With a daily budget of 10$ you can easily send traffic to your website or any other channel used and make incredible numbers in sales.

Current changes that are taking place in marketing world.

Newsletters - LinkedIn (Social media platform destined for business purposes)

News Media – Twitter

TV and Radio – YouTube & Podcasts

Intranet – Podcasts

Surveys – Forums

The expression of "social media " can be separated in the fallowing :

- Social = it's clear that it's destined to interact with people and serve a medium populated with activity from other people
- Media = Media it's more related to audio – visual, written content, infographic, displaying the content publishing on the web.

It can be percept as a medium were conversation can take place between people and gives you access to people all around the world. Basically to the primary function of creating and distributing forms of content social media can be very effective in developing brand awareness, everything that has to do with developing a personal brand, establishing your image as a recognized brand and scaling it up. Another function of social media is networking, as I said you can interact with people all around the world, connecting with potential business partners.

I've separated those two because at some level they can be quite different even though both of them are finally directed to creating and improving contact with the person that it's buying. Looking back, at a big brand's point of view, the social media platforms enable for all of as engagement with customers in real time, a Facebook campaign can create results in a matter of days even hours strengthening their need in today's marketing and advertising industry.

The benefits of using social media

Here we can go with a long list of benefits to using social media:

- It's free, you don't have to pay anything to register, at least none of the big platforms like Facebook, Twitter, Instagram, Pinterest, YouTube, LinkedIn. Due to the fact that platforms are interested in getting people to register on their website I don't thing that any taxes will be percept for registration not now or in future. The more people that

are using a platform the better and Facebook it's the Leader of this chapter
- You can reach a larger group of people and more targeted on what you are interested in selling or advertising, can be more focused on you niche and not losing money reaching people that you are not interested in(taking in consideration that you understand what you are doing).
- Gives you real-time feedback, you get in the shortest period of time updates on how your campaign/campaigns are going any possibility to interact with people that are willing to buy from you
- It's the most powerful communication tool available due to the fact that audience on TV, Radio, written media(newspaper, magazines) are slowly but surely getting smaller

First choices of social media platforms

The most obvious choices are represented by Facebook, Instagram, LinkedIn Twitter(in my opinion potential that Instagram has it's not even tapped yet and all the possibilities that this social media platform can offer and also the slowly but surely Twitter's fall). We can use YouTube which it's without any questions replacing the TV and Radio. The days of picking up a pen and write a message don't really exist anymore.

Below you will have a little explanation of the main social networking websites :

LinkedIn – Business to business and business to consumer networking

Facebook – social and business to customer website

Twitter – Small bite-size messages information's

YouTube – Video- broadcasting website

Google+   - Business to business and business to consumer website

How is this going to help you to grow your business?

Simple :

- Create attractive posts
- Listen to the voice of the customers
- Build your business network
- Impress them with your originality

Benefits of networking online

The benefits of networking online are more than you can imagine:

- The fact that's free, you have access 24/7, 365 days per year
- You can access people all over the world
- It's effective and simple

- It's a less pressured medium, without having the pressure of time limit
- You can do it from the comfort of your own home
- It's easier than ever to find mentors
- It's easier than ever to create masterminds, to improve businesses, to learn from other's experiences and the list goes on and on.

Ideas for your content

Going through a couple of social media platforms I came with the fallowing topics for posts.

Facebook:

- Funny videos or funny pictures
- Memes or anything that can bring a smile on somebody's face
- Blog posts from your website, updates about your company activity or your personal activity
- Announcements about new releases or future events that you intend to host
- Interesting news attractive content that engages people's curiosity to read more

LinkedIn :

Due to the fact, that LinkedIn has a business look and it's created for that specific reason your content should follow the same thing, respecting that:

- Posts about latest updates in the industry you are in right now
- Shares on what your future business partners might be interested in
- Writing articles about your business results, how you improved your activity, and here I'm referring to sales, ROI, anything that can deliver value and quality information's to people

Twitter:

Well when It comes to Twitter we have a mixture of possibilities, it's still a strong name out there, that it's sure but popularity it's going down, people are being limited by the number of characters that a "tweet" can have and how short it's the information that they can deliver to people, I consider Twitter more like a "Mood Update", every couple of hours I'm informing my followers how I'm feeling and what I'm doing basically for those that are not familiar with this platform.

- Tweet what you are currently doing
- Tweet short videos

- Tweet links to articles
- Tweet other people tweets, retweet
- Comment on others tweet with your own content

YouTube

The most popular platform for uploading videos, released at the same time with Vimeo but more popular due to how simple is to use it and for how many possibilities are to add ads.

- Upload videos about your activity
- Upload funny people
- Upload frequently, your viewers are interested in how often do you post, they want lots and lots of content to consume, you start playing so play till the end

What makes people share posts online?

Well, where we can say that it's an art to getting people's attention and also to convince them to share your content. It's a level of implication and investment that they are doing in that moment. People love to share things, funny things, interesting things, everything that catches your attention.

Triggers are what makes a person "click" in their mind usually. It's called trigger, some kind of information/content that resonates with the person in cause and it will make her reacting. Maybe that check-in at a pizza restaurant, maybe your photo with a view from a beautiful apartment, maybe a picture with a smile, anything can be considered a trigger for your audience and your job is to test in, in major lines model other businesses social media profiles and try to see what creates engagement and test out variations to your content to find what makes people to "click".

When we FEEL we share, the emotion it's being implied in this process. The "click" it's being made primarily for the emotional investment that it's being made. For a second let's take YouTube videos, short or long videos with specific content create that emotion in the person that it's watching, THE MAIN IDEA it's how your viewer identifies emotionally with your content based on their own self-image. For example, if you are producing videos on social anxiety, how to get rid of social anxiety and anything related to this subject take in consideration the variety of emotions that your viewer it's experimenting. "Click" on your content is being made by identifying with what you are publishing and the emotional state that YOU are influencing when they are consuming your content.

Giving value always will be rewarded! You can come across on something really useful, people will reward you, basically what you are doing is to acquire their attention in order to make them share your content.

Tell a story!

When you were just a little kid you were looking forward to the moment when your parents were reading you a story before going to sleep, you were listening to the story and imagine everything, the action, how the characters are looking, creating a fantasy in your mind and thinking about how awesome was what you heard and how much you would like to do or be like in the person in the story in case you identified with the character.

The same thing applies also to the mind of an adult, either you are a child or a grown man you will always enjoy hearing stories, well actually your mind will enjoy that more than you. Creating a story in the mind of your audience will make then act like little kids, thinking back to what they saw on your page, thinking and imagining with your product, let's say or smiling back at your funny photo, the good or bad sensation created by the story that you told will make that person to share it with a friend because, as we talked earlier of the identification in a form or another with your activity on social media, and this is how it's done folks. No big schemes being involved, just work, consistency and start planning with constant adjustments.

Rules of engagement

So here you have a couple of rules and guidelines that create engagement, position you in a good way and are pretty simple to be followed:

- Never swear, people will see that you are being reactive and will tax you, be careful about that

- Don't get your company in disputes, don't get yourself involved in scandals or anything that can create a bad image to your company, ok publicity it's still publicity good or bad, but be careful about that, if viewers or better say your future customers don't trust your company, your brand they won't give you a second chance
- Don't argue with competitors, try to be better than them, try to compete in a good and respectful manner but don't argue with competitors
- Deal with all complaints as they were just advice. If somebody complains about something then for sure it's just giving you feedback, something it's lacking and in this way you can get back to drawing board and improve the quality to your product or service. What do you think about that? I'm pretty sure that people will appreciate

Keep an eye on profitability

Social media it's great but posting content it's a form of investment, keep an eye on how profitable it's your investment over time, if over a long period of time you don't have any returns, well then something it's not good. Your final goal it's to create profit, a business can't exist without cash flow, can't exist without profit, then it's an ONG. Good thing it's that platforms like Facebook give you tools, Facebook Insights it's a free tool offered by Facebook to you. For example let's say if your majority of your fans are being females between 18 – 25 than use that information in your advantage to post something that will engage then and finally to see in your sales.

Get bigger ROI

It's very important for your business to determine the ROI (return on investment) that you want to have. Below you have a couple of ways in which you can determine and also improve your business ROI:

- How engaged is your stuff in relationship with your clients
- What have you learned from your customers and how they helped you to get your business better
- Did you manage to deliver the best product or service to your clients?

Conclusions :

Now you understand how social media is helping you to develop your business and how important is to know how to use it for you to get bigger ROI and scale up as fast as possible. Determination and ambition will be also a key factor in your success. The knowledge it's just potential power if it's not used so be careful on what you pay attention.

Chapter 2 - Facebook marketing domination for newbies and advanced marketers

In this chapter will cover the following :

- How to create content for your Facebook page
- What type of content to post and what creates authority
- Managing your fans and their expectations
- Facebook ads and how they should look like

Facebook was originally created in 2004 having the purpose to be used inside the university campus, created by Mark Zuckerberg as we all know. From 2004 till now Facebook suffered a lot of changes and updates that make it the website that we all know today.

Short facts about the website

- In 2014 Facebook got over 1 billion users all over the world
- The average user on Facebook has over 100 friends, it's over 20 years old and it's pretty aware of the internet era that he lives right now

- More than 60% of the users are active and log in on a daily basis
- It's the fastest website when it comes to growth rate

Marketing on Facebook can be a challenge for sure that no question about that but if you are keeping everything simple it can be one of the easiest ways to make money online. Marketers all over the world look at the possibilities that Facebook offers in special on local marketing by setting Personal pages, Business Pages, Communities and so on. You can also can get real time feedback, reactions to your campaign and more tools and information's that you can imagine.

Personal Facebook Page

A personal Facebook page can be used by individuals for personal pages, it's the most used type of account by individuals on Facebook to keep in touch with friends and relatives. Even though it's a personal page in can be easily be used for "social selling" in case you are having business that requires selling B2C . This method it's more used on LinkedIn than Facebook due to the fact that LinkedIn it's build with this purpose and more to gather more business people and Facebook more for socializing and sharing content.

A couple facts about running your personal Facebook account for business purposes :

- You are risking your account to be closed, it's against Facebook terms and conditions to use personal accounts instead of business accounts
- Already have a Facebook account
- To be friend with that person you want to get in conversation or at least to have common friends
- To be sure not to have more than 5000 friends, Facebook allows you to have maximum 5000 ,after that you will have to fallow that person

Community Page

Community pages should not be avoided for sure, are very good to collect lots of people under the same umbrella of interest, a little bit harder to get a sale from this type of audience but not impossible. Communities are created on different topics and subjects, ideas or even political interests.

Group Page

A group page it's another option to consider, if you are creating a golf club, racing club or pool club this will be a great choice. A couple of reasons to consider opening this type of page :

- You can send e-mails to the members, that is representing a good way to collect their e-mail addresses for future affiliate marketing campaigns
- You can discuss with members in privacy without violating Facebook's terms of use
- Group pages will not be seen by Google so you don't have to worry about being spammed

Business page

When it comes to the most frequent choice that marketers make, business pages are the most common one. It's practical, it's easy to administrate it's easy to create and to advertise. Couple points:

- Page can be easily be seen on Google
- It's a good choice either if you are a small business or medium size business
- Updates for your fans are being delivered in the shortest time
- Friends of your fans will see on their newsfeed the posts, likes and comments

Set up a business page

When you finally decide to get a Facebook page and you are ready to take your business to the next level you will have 2 options for you to open a page :

1. First one and the most common way is to open a page by using your personal Facebook account. All you have to do it's to click "Create Page" from the drop-down menu on your profile page.
2. The second way its to go to https://www.facebook.com/pages/create and again fallow the same instructions.

I can say that are advantages and disadvantages for every method that you use:

- If you create a business page from your personal profile you will have full access to that page to make any updates you want
- You can create admins to you page so you won't be the only administrator taking car of the page. That will allow you to take care on more sides of your business. The ability to schedule posts it's another fact very important in your business development.
- If you choose to run a business-only account there will be less functionalities and more restrictions to what you can do, my recommendation will be to use a personal account when you are opening a business page.

Category choice

Good! Congrats for being here! Now that we got over that step lets take a look at some of the categories that we have to chose:

1. Local business or Place : this one I recommend for pizza, restaurant, shops, café, bars and so on to chose. Basically any type of business that will probably will have a physical location and your client will require to go in person, but it's not a demand. It's very easy to be found by clients while they are using their smartphones
2. Artist, band or public figure : as the name of the category says you will chose this category more if you want to expose yourself as a public person, it will not be used for selling shoes if your name it's on this one because will represent you. It's a good way to start your music career or your politician career
3. Brand, product or organization: another category that it's being used a lot, let's say you have a brand of T-Shirts, this one it's a good choice for your business.

DON'T PANIC if you chose the wrong category! You can change it later, depends on you what you see the most relevant to your audience! Now that you choose the type of page that you want to have all you need to do now it's to fill up the basic details like name, nickname, description an get your first 100 page fans.

Customize your page!

A key element in attracting more people on your page it's represented by graphics. Add a cover photo on your page will make a big visual impact. For example a good cover photo can be an image representing an offer that you have right now on your website! People will be tented to consume visual content more than written content due to the fact that its more easy to understand it and also you can get the idea faster! Another element very important it's your profile photo! It's the first thing that a visitor will see when its going to enter on your page. Your profile photo has to be something representative to your business, easy to remember, easy to understand : your logo! It's the only association that a customer will make to your brand or place when it's going to think about it. Take a look at the examples that are below with some big brands on the market.

Here are 2 examples from some big brands out there like Nike, having the logo on their profile picture and also the restaurant McDonald's.

You may have more companies that you need to administrate, no worries. A single account it's enough to administrate all of then on a single Facebook page. If you have a café or you have a restaurant or a brand of socks you can have for each one a business page under the same umbrella. This makes your personal Facebook page like a portal.

Content Plan

Fallow your content plan! Posting on your page it's something that you are going to do active or the person that you give access as an administrator.

Post as much as possible on your wall, don't forget to have a limit with your posts, be decent as we talk earlier and in case you didn't created a content plan create one and test it, if it doesn't work than change it and try again till you find what your audience likes more! For a better understanding about how to analyze the situation and to create that plan I suggest you to think about the following:

- What content you usually consume and you like and think that you can produce the same type of quality?
- What type of content do you prefer to consume? Visual, written or audio content?
- What can you do to be more different than your competition?
- What affiliates can you find for your business to get exposure on Facebook or other platforms

Your content plan it's "what makes you or breaks you". Having a well structured plan will make the biggest difference in the way you acquire visitors to your page. By going to "war" without having a plan will not bring you any benefit. Take your time and to see what your audience really likes to consume, to develop the content plan.

Let's take at the fallowing example:

1. Pizzeria : Start by taking a look at the most appropriate competitors that you have and how they prefer to do their marketing:
- What are their favorites channels to market
- How much are investing in advertising
- How their location it's looking
- What are saying clients bad about them

Outside posts on your business page!

Should you let your fans to post on your page? This is an interesting question! When you are looking at big brands or some of the biggest celebrities they do not allow fans to post on their Facebook wall. Why? It helps them to mention a clean image online. Due to the way you project your image in online medium letting fans post on your Facebook page can make big differences in the way a new visitor will judge you. Seeing fights, seeing obscene words, people advertising and the list can go on and on won't not benefit at wall your evolution in online.

How to engage with people?

Comments. Reply to as many comments as possible, take care of their needs. Reply not to positive comments but also to negative comments. Often people with post more negative comments than positive comments. Deleting comments will just impact you negatively, TRY as much as possible to reply to them giving them positive and good information's and try not to be reactive to them. Also to measure how negative comments are appearing and also what type of content, schedule your posts on Facebook and the type of posts that you are going to do.

Facebook Ads

Facebook ads is a subject very important. Here we enter in the world of paid Advertising.

Facebook ads are pretty complex to do proper, type of photo used in ad, text included, call to action option and so on. The most important things that we must take care of are the fallowing:

- Location that you choose for your ad. For example if you choose to target around the region where your business is located and get a specific reach to your audience or if you prefer to target a hole country or more countries in your campaign. Result will be definitely influenced by the budget that you intend to spend per campaign.

- Demographics – here we are going to talk a little bit of the characteristics of your customer like the sex. What is your customer sex? Man or Woman? What age has your customer? Its 16 years or 36 years old? And the list can continue
- Interests – Interests are very important let's say you are selling a baseball jacket and you are creating an Ad. It will be good idea to add to you interest baseball, your customer might be interested in baseball on general for the fact that he is looking for a baseball jacket, be specific about interest not just the big keywords that are coming in your mind. Go as specific as possible but also include big niches not just the small ones.
- Connections - the users that you are targeting what are the most connected in their life, what type of information's prefer to consume on a daily basis and how related is with the content and with the interest that is targeted.

Once you went though this process you will have a better understanding of how to create a Facebook Ad and how to think about this process. Once you got a clear idea of how your customer is looking like, what are his interests, age and sex you are almost done. Answer to the fallowing questions:

1. Who are you trying to reach and what is your target market?

   Even though we have covered this topic above there are still a couple of things that have to be discussed about this subject. What is the occupation of your target? Is a 40 years old single mom recently divorced looking for way to keep looking young and fresh? I'm pretty sure that it's pretty clear what we have to look for now. Keep in mind that in the title you have 25 characters and 133 in the body of your ad to fill with text so chose carefully and wisely what keywords you are going to use.

2. What is your final goal of your ad?
   Even though the reasons may be obvious, I strongly suggest you think about what is your final goal? I made this mistake in past, I thought that only creating a Facebook Ad will be the biggest thing that I can do in my marketing and this is totally WRONG! If you are in business your final goal should be to make profit (by honorable and ethical ways) but not every ad that you create won't have the goal to create sales in the first phase. You may create ads that the only purpose will be to bring likes to your Facebook page constant so you can get more trust in online world.
   Think clear about your goal. You may have ads that only reason would be to make customers to buy with a single click(but also think about how to save that customer that you spent once money to acquire – CPA – cost per acquisition topic right here)
   If your goal is to generate more brand exposure getting more likes will be best choice to look for.

3. What is your budget for the ad?
   How Facebook Ads work its pretty simple, you will set a daily budget that Facebook will use. Obvious the more you spend the visible will be the results and you will have more data to compare and get a better understanding of the results that you got out of the campaign.

i. Calculate your total budget for this Ad and how much are you ready to spend in this campaign. Having a fixed budget will help you a lot, don't start your campaign without calculating all your costs to know what you are getting yourself into. Ads budget are calculated daily so you will have to think first on how much you intend to spend per day on your Ad. You can spend as little as 3$ per day or even 30$. The more budget you have the more results (is suppose) to have.

ii. For how long do you want to have the ad running? 5 days, 1 week, 2 weeks? If you don't have a set period you risk to lose customers. Running an Ad for a period of time that is too short will not benefit you at all or running an Ad for a longer period without being effective will just consume your budget without giving you any results resulting in a low ROI.

iii. Keep a constant eye on your Ad. From Facebook Insights you can constantly monitor your Ad see how effective is the way you configured your campaign. You can change Ad while running BUT my recommendation will be not to do that just if you invested more than you should in the campaign and you are risking to loose a big junk of money. I strongly suggest you to start testing Ads with small budgets till you find which one works best for you. With experience you won't fear that your ad won't work, you will be preoccupied more with optimizing.

iv. Create a simple story – most of the ads that I see working on Facebook usually are looking like a simple story. You will have to be pretty straight forward with your intend: this is my product, this is how is going to benefit you and here you can buy it. Make it look like something simple to understand and sell it more through benefits that can bring into your life than the price. People will often ask for the price even people working in sales and that it's not the most relevant aspect when creating the story and the fantasy to your client. The emotion's what will create that drive inside him to buy it: the cover, the package. The fact that your brand is associated with his favorite musician or actor.

Conclusion

Facebook has become more than a social media platform, it's integrated into our life in more ways than we can imagine. A little comparison that I like to make sometimes it's becoming more and more like "Skynet" in the movie series "Terminator" but hopefully without the bad aspects. Constant updates are keeping the users engaged and the number of benefits that are offering to the normal users but also to marketers is making Facebook absolutely irresistible not to use.

Chapter 3 - Twitter marketing domination for newbies and advanced marketers

What will talk about in this chapter?

- Steps to set up your Twitter account and how to go get into Twitter
- How to use Twitter, tweets and retweets
- What are the tools that Twitter offers and how to use them
- And much other information's about Twitter marketing and Twitter impact in social media world

Twitter it's a well-known social media platform a little bit different than Facebook or any other platform that we talked till now. Before getting into all the good stuff about Tweeter lets take a short look at some general information's about this platform:

- Domain name : www.twitter.com
- It looks and works like a "mini blog" ,short and constant updates about what you are doing

- It has a limit of 140 characters per tweet
- A message it's called "tweet"
- Twitter was founded in 2006, 2 years after Facebook
- It has over 70% of their users active every month
- Over the time over 500 billion of tweets have been sent

Twitter

Twitter a social networking platform that been part of social media evolution over time. 2006 was the year when was founded by Jack Dorsey, Noah Glass, Biz Stone, Evan Williams. Over the time the company evolved a lot even developed and acquired a couple of success subsidiaries like Vine(a video hosting service where users can share video clips) and Periscope (a live video streaming developed for iOS and Android smartphones). Taking a look at some stats it looks like the company made in revenue US $2.52 billions in 2016 with almost 4000 employees(3,898). In Alexa rank it takes the position 16, with a decrease due to recent events(losing popularity). The website it's written in Java, Ruby and JavaScript programming languages.

"What's happening?" It's the question that greets you when you are "tweeting" one of the strong points of the platform it's the easiness which you can send messages and interact with other people.

Businesses saw immediate the advantages of using a platform like this to keep clients updated constantly about what new products or services. The business side of this platform it's something very important and the reason of taking Twitter in discussion. Even though recently the platform it's losing popularity slowly it's still a pylon in online networking world and very effective for online businesses.

As time went by and more and more people started using Twitter individuals saw the opportunity to bring in attention small businesses and develop incredible opportunities and business models based on this platform. Depending on the business model that your business it's based on will vary also the social media platforms that you will you in the way you market your business. Let's get into basics of Twitter and how to use this platform for getting followers, getting traffic and to go to the next level with your business.

Let's set up a Twitter account

Like the process of setting up a Facebook account, setting up a Twitter account it's pretty simple and straightforward, on Twitter website you will find a sign up form. Enter your full name, e-mail and password and you are ready to go.

On the homepage you will see a couple of tabs like : Home,

Notifications, Messages and a search bar. On the left side you will see your profile with the total number of tweets that you posed, your number of followers and the number of people that you follow.

On your **Profile page** you can easily decide if you will build it for personal purposes or business purposes.

Taking for example Coca-cola business page it's pretty important to take some note:

- It's pretty similar to Facebook business page
- Profile photo it's the logo of the company like on any other platform(for brand recognition purposes)
- The cover photo it's used for advertisement purposes for new products, services or promotions.
- The company colors are everywhere on the page also for brand recognition

Having those things in consideration I'll always guide myself after the big brands for creating a page that will probably attract visitors.

Find your audience

Now that you built your page and you added your company logo as profile picture, a promo banner as cover photo and filled in the rest of information's in your profile like the company interest, company location and how it going to impact the world lets start working on getting our first followers that will become our first clients also.

Going by a general rule of reciprocity usually people follow reciprocally follow each other friends, family or relatives usually they follow each other back. The same principle applies to businesses. I strongly suggest starting your marketing campaign on Twitter by first following your friends and relatives on Twitter and as soon as possible to start following people that are interested in the product or service that you are selling. In most cases they will follow back just for the simple fact that they are interested in what you are selling not especially in your product, or not for now. If they won't buy now that doesn't mean they won't buy after a period of time.

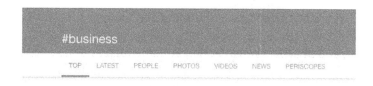

This is how a search with the" #business" looks like. After this search you will easily get a list of people that have included #business in their post and you can contact then with offers or just to include them in your tweet so you will let them know about your business.

As you can see in this print screen there are a couple of categories that people really look up to like: top, latest or people.

Exercise 1: Make a search with the keyword that you are interested to find people and make a list with the results that you get. You will be amazed by the information's that Twitter will give you. I consider this to be a biggest advantage that Twitter has instead of Facebook. Even though you can make a hashtag search on Facebook, I don't consider to have the same quality of result like Twitter has. Thumbs up Twitter for that!

Exercise 2: Follow 100 people on Twitter and see how many of them will follow you back. This is the first method that I recommend for getting your first followers.

! Please be careful, you don't want Twitter to see you as spamming that will attract the consequence of deactivating your account. Take a look on some actions that I consider that should be avoided when working on Twitter:

- Sending a large number of replies to your messages
- Creating a big following in a period of time that is too short
- Marketing pornography or any obscene content on your Twitter account

Those I consider being the most important aspects to take in consideration so you won't look like you are spamming in the eyes of Twitter or that you have a fake account.

Impress people

1. Retweet ! Another way to improve the number of followers that you have is to retweet others tweets. Pretty simple and people love to find out about quality information's, right?
Retweeting says to the people that you found a good information, like a photo, song or text that has value and by retweeting you are putting that person post in attention and also yours. People will appreciate it and will have the intent to follow you just for the fact that you are sharing good and valuable informations according to their interests.

2. Respect your followers! Let's talk about something that sometimes it's avoided in sales. Nobody likes to be sold on anything either we talk about selling a physical product or something simple and non-tangible like an idea. Gain people's trust by giving . Give them lots and lots of free and valuable information's. As human beings we tend to trust entities that won't ask nothing in return of their service and will feel obligated to give something in return as a result that we have been helped to go a little closer to our goals or just got a smile on face.

3. Create a relationship! Let people know that you are the CEO of the company or a person in a management position that people can get in touch with. Nobody it's satisfied to talk with customer support, people know that customer support it's the lowest hierarchical position that they can get in touch with for their requirements. Having a person from C-Level to talk with

make the customers feel like they are really appreciated any somebody its really looking for their needs and somebody REALLY CARES about their problems. Listen to them, really create a relationship with the person that it's buying your products and really love the business you are in! People feel when you are true to themselves and not trying to scam anybody. How do you create a relationship with customers? Reply to their messages, let them know on the official Twitter page of your company the position you have in the company and they can get in touch with you. Indeed will be very time consuming at first to reply and talk back with customers but for sure will pay back!

4. Scale up! Indeed the start may be slow and will have a lot to work but as soon as you get some friction on your Twitter page all you have to do it's just to scale up! Your first 100 followers or 1000 followers will be a little harder to get but once you got over that a number you will see that the growth rate will just improve and improve. Be active with your posts, I strongly suggest you to post regularly every 3-4 hours daily with information's about products but also general information's related to the niche you are in.

FACTS

- \# (hashtags) let you have a conversation about a particular topic for example #LeBron or let's say #grind. Simple by putting a #(hashtag) other people will be able to find you on that topic and you also can find other people.
- Retweet as often as possible
- @replies are visible to everyone visiting your twitter page
- You can have a private conversation on chat with different people if you follow them and they also follow you

Auto Following tools

At some point will become pretty difficult to follow lots and lots of people but it's good thing that we have tools that we can use for those situations. You can use tools for auto follow to use base on your interests that will do that automatically for you. Bellow you will have a list of tools that I recommend to take a look on:

1. Tweet Adder

Tweet Adder is the most powerful software that lets you auto-follow your twitter followers along with a lot of other powerful features that can help you to boost Twitter Marketing.

2. Refollow

Refollow is another Twitter Automation Tool that lets you follow all your new followers instantly. This tool is having a lot of other options also.

3. Pluggio – Tame Twitter

Pluggio is not just an auto-follow tool, it is much more. Along with auto-following your new followers, it lets you add multiple twitter accounts, schedule auto tweet, browsing your friends' popular tweets.

Chapter 4 - Instagram truth revealed and how to properly promote your product

What will talk about in this chapter?

- Step by step how to set up your Instagram account
- How to create a following on Instagram
- What is required to sell and how to sell
- Selling tools that you can use
- Targeting the right audience

Instagram is a well-known platform for mobile photo-sharing developed in special for mobile devices to share pictures and videos, basically just visual content. Pretty unique platform when it was released in 2010 for the fact that it was only platforming back then dedicated just for photo sharing. Users have the possibility to add filters to their photos, edit them directly from their photo application. Instagram's mobile app its one of the best photo editing tools out right now on the market. In June 2013 Instagram added support for videos, allowing users to upload short videos of 15 seconds. Now you can upload videos up to 60 seconds.

- Domain name : www.instagram.com
- It's a continuous page lets you scroll down, every new post it's being displayed on the homepage
- It has only 3 pages: Discover people, Notifications and My profile
- Photos are being found by #(hashtags)
- It's available in 25 languages and it's one of the most popular social media platforms at the moment
- It's developed by Facebook

Instagram

Instagram has originally been created by Kevin Systrom and Mike Krieger. Even though was originally released in June 2010 by December 2010 the platform already had registered one million users. Instagram showed even from release day potential to become a big player on social media game and by June 2011, exactly one year after release had 5 million users. In December 2014 Instagram officials announced that they got over 300 million users getting on their website on a monthly basis and now they have over 600 million monthly active users. Instagram it's betting big!

Mark Zuckerberg saw the potential that the application has and as a result in April 2012 Facebook acquired Instagram for approximately $1 Billion US Dollars. The deal was a great one due to the fact that Instagram continued to grow at an incredible rate. After releasing Instagram stories in August 2016 it's preconized that it's going to go over the main competitor , Snapchat, in 2017 and years that are about to come.

Set up an Instagram account

   Pretty easy to set up an Instagram account. Go to www.instagram.com and there you will see a sign up form that asks you for your e-mail address, your full name, username and password. After completing those fields you are good to go. The news feed will be the first thing that will appear, empty due to the fact that you haven't followed any person yet and your profile obviously empty for the same reason.

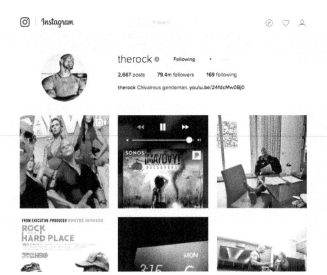

As any other platform you can use Instagram for individual purposes or for business purposes. On this platform it's not any difference on how you create your account, just one type of account that can be made. The only difference it's on how you market your profile.

As we talked in previous chapters everything starts with creating brand awareness on the platform that you are market on business.

Be careful! Depending on the business that you are developing right now will vary also the social media platform that you will use. Most of the businesses out there are marketing on all social media platform. If you are not a public person or a big brand, I don't advice you to start creating accounts on all the social media platforms. I advise you to use Twitter more for services and Instagram more for selling physical products.

How to sell physical products on Instagram

When it comes to selling physical products on Instagram having beautiful photos it's the key to attracting people on your page. Everything comes to quality videos and quality images that deliver the feeling and the sensation that your customer wants to have by watching it.

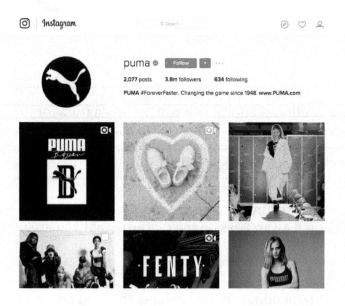

Lets take for example Puma's Instagram page. On the profile you will see Puma' logo that will help for brand recognition. The description of the page must be as direct as possible. Your customer won't spend time to understand what are you doing, you must capture him in a fraction of a second. Usually website and a couple of words about domain of activity should be enough. Your Instagram bio should include also your @nickname to make him know pretty easy how to find you as a business and also an e-mail address.

Let's talk about Instagram posts

Posting on your business account it's a little bit different than your personal account. The quality of pictures matters a lot more than your personal account. People will judge your products quality after the photos that you post.

Marketing is in photos, selling your product it's in photos. Getting your visitor to actually click on your website it's in your photos and photos quality.

Let's talk a little bit about how your photos should look like:

1. Lighting: As mush as possible try to have natural lighting in your photos to make your product look as good as possible. Make sure to include your product in front of a window for natural lighting.
2. Background: I can't stress enough about the importance of background. You can put your product on a white background, exterior background including people or objects and so on. It's important how it makes you FEEL when you are looking at that photo. The most important thing it's the emotion that you can wake up in the person that is looking at your photo.

Taking, for example, a picture from a well known brand like Daniel Wellington. They sell very beautiful watches. As you can see in this photo, a person taking a selfie somewhere on an island having an incredible view. Part of their marketing on Instagram it's to position their products on backgrounds like this that can make you feel a positive emotion related to what you are seeing. The watch it's a secondary element in this photo, barely visible on the hand of the person that taking the picture.

Instagram Toolkit

Every photo needs to be edited, if you are not getting photos done by a photographer and you are doing photos by yourself I strongly suggest you to get on your device a couple of applications to edit photos and make them look better:

- Camera + : Great app for photo editing for iOS
- VSCO : I totally recommend it for how simple is the interface and also friendly, available on iOS and Android
- Photoshop (mobile version) : we can't talk about photo editing without Photoshop, great on your computer, great on your mobile device also. The features are limited due to the fact that you are on the mobile version but still good to have and to use it. Available on iOS and Android

Best time for posting

When it comes to social media I can say for sure that there is a window for posting when you have better chances to get the viewers attention. Just studying a couple of statistics the best time that I also found for Instagram posts I've discovered to be between 6 to 7 P.M. for weekends and for the rest of the week after 6 PM when most of the people are getting out from their job. Usually people are checking their social media on their phone while stuck in traffic or while they are going home with the bus.

Morning posts are also important. Most of the people have 9 to

5 jobs, it's a fact. Usually people are checking their social media as second or third thing in the morning starting with 7 am.

Use # in your advantage

Like Twitter, Instagram it's very focused on # hashtags. I can say that # hashtags are more important on Instagram than Twitter because on every post you can include # to pump your post in the photos that are released on Instagram. After watching a lot of Instagram posts getting likes, comments and lots of traffic I can divide the # in the following:

1. Tags that have the purpose to sell you as they get your attention like:
- #shop, #buy, #4sale, #getItToday, #discount, #limitedOffer

2. Tags that have the purpose to describe the item in the post or events that took place in that photo or emotional relevant actions or object like:
- #bestday, #grind, #justStarted, #fitnessMotivations, #BarcelonaTrip

3. Tags that are general and are being specific about the post like:
- #fashion, #curly, #blue, #pizza

In my experience for best results I advise your to use # from all tree categories when just starting out and test a lot, test everything that comes into your mind. Usually a list of 10-20-30 tags on every post will help you to boost your posts and combined with a good timing when you are posting should boost your profile a lot.

Affiliate marketing on Instagram!

Indeed a business profile has the exact purpose for selling your own products but nowadays having a big following on your personal account can be what you really need to make business. Having a strong following on your personal account can serve even more than having a business account. You can promote others products and earn a commission as an affiliate on each sale. The big advantage of affiliate marketing it's that you don't have to worry about product creation or shipping or customer support or any other problem related to the product itself. All you have to do it's just to sale it!

Advanced Instagram marketing

Taking care of an Instagram account and marketing it properly it's now difficult but can be challenging for sure! Frequency in posting is very important if you want to have success on this platform. Posting 3 times per week won't be enough to get many followers. I recommend you to post daily and to have about 2 posts per day , in the morning and in the evening.

In this "battle" I recommend you to equip with the right tools. In this big world of tools and services and apps it becomes harder and harder to find the right ones and now to get lost into using every tool out there and not get the best result. Below you have a list of a couple of tools that I recommend:

1. Hashtag research – finding the best hashtags can be quite challenging. Tagstagram I totally recommend for getting trending tags and help you in this constant fight of getting the best hashtags that are basically keywords
2. Planning your posts – For posting lots and lots of phots I recommend you to try a tool for planning your posts. I've saw accounts with over 10k posts and at some level becomes pretty hard to make that many posts on a daily basis. For that I recommend your Latergram
3. Profile Growth – Following it's very important and having people follow you back it's the engine of your business when you are just starting out. Liking commenting and following can be a lot improved with a tools for growth like Instagress with automates everything. A paid tool that definitely helps in your journey.

Conclusion

Thank you again for downloading this book!

I hope this book was able to help you to understand how social media work and how affects us and also enjoyed the book!

The next step is to be sure that you fully understand the information, also apply it and read it as frequently as necessary.

Finally, if you enjoyed this book, then I'd like to ask you for a favour, would you be kind enough to leave a review for this book on Amazon? It'd be greatly appreciated!

If you enjoyed the the this book check out other releases that you might like:

Data Analytics: Essentials to master Data Analytics and get your business to the next level

SEO: The definitive guide to keyword research